Many Way To Make Cash Fast

Chapter:1

need a little more money in a hurry? you can sense pressure when you want to make money speedy, however you do have alternatives for getting it completed. those encompass promoting items, doing odd jobs, and locating cash in overlooked ways. these techniques may also or won't be dependable long-term, but while you want to make a few cash in some hours or days, they're your satisfactory shot.

sell belongings you now not need.

 A quick and smooth manner to make a few cash is to sell precious, excessive-demand items. go searching your private home for normally-bought objects you no longer need, consisting of:

CDs

DVDs

Books

Musical gadgets

Collectible toys

electronic gadget (computers, tablets, televisions, audio system, etc.)

Smartphones

Video games

jewelry

Crafts

Unused present cards (these may be sold on various web sites, or redeemed immediately at Coinstar kiosks)

search for approaches to sell your gadgets. you could deal with selling your objects to human beings you understand, in-character to clients, or online. depending on where you live, any of those methods might be a manner of making a sale fast.

backyard income

Flea markets

on line websites such as eBay

"on the market" postings (on a bulletin board, in a newspaper, or on an online classifieds board like Craigslist)

Pawn stores

on-line retail web sites like Amazon or AbeBooks.com will now and again pay quickly for popular objects like books, DVDs, electronics, and smartphones. these web sites may rate a small price or percentage of your earnings.

exchange-in at shops; a few will purchase objects like used dressmaker garb, CDs and data, or books instant.

Set a competitive fee in your items.

deciding how a whole lot to promote your stuff for can be hard. but, in case you charge items at half of what anyone might have the ability to buy them for everywhere else, you are more likely to make a short sale. when you are trying to make cash in a hurry, this is probably your precedence.

Don't sell gadgets for a deeply discounted price until you really need cash in a rush.

promote matters to pedestrians. Entrepreneurial sorts sell things like bloodless liquids on warm days or warm nuts in iciness. This approach can be specifically beneficial if you installation a gap near a wearing occasion, park, etc. You'll want to have a small sum of money to make investments within the product, however then you may sell it at a miles better go back and make some brief coins.

as an example, say you buy a multi-percent of 20 water bottles for $five. If then you promote water to pedestrians for $1 a bottle, then you can make $20, leaving you with an common income of $15.

check laws for your place and make certain that it is legal to sell gadgets on this manner.

Be cautious if you are trying to sell matters in high site visitors zones.

sell scavenged valuables. if you have a metal detector, or even simply a very good eye, visit public locations in which human beings are probably to drop some thing disregarded (consisting of parks, beaches, and purchasing regions), and search for money, rings and different precious items. This method isn't very dependable, however you simply would possibly get fortunate and be capable of find something you may sell fast for coins.

Chapter:2

promote your hair. if your hair is healthy, untreated, and lengthy enough, you could sell it for up to loads of dollars. There are now on line marketplaces to help you promote your hair, further to salons or different centers on your area that can be interested bytired buying hair.

Hair up to 10 inches regularly sells for much less than $one hundred dollars. as the duration of the hair increases, so does the fee. Hair over 30 inches lengthy might also promote for $960 or extra.

sell blood or donate plasma.

Plasma is part of blood, and the manner of extracting it is much like donating blood: your blood is drawn, the plasma is separated, and the crimson blood cells are again to your body. legal guidelines might not technically allow you to sell your plasma, but you may be compensated on your time spent donating. within the u.s.a., you may make worn-outapproximately $two hundred a month by using registering with a plasma middle close to you.

normally, you have to be among 18 and 65 and in excellent fitness to donate plasma.

Many plasma donation facilities will compensate you with a pre-loaded gift card.

promote sperm. Sperm donors could make doubtlessly make numerous hundred dollars a month, and the payment is generally quick. however, you must by and large be tall, educated, and healthful to grow to be a donor. you could find a donation middle close to you, sign up, and begin as quickly as possible.

return bottles and cans for money back. In a few states, you may get 5 or 10 cents in line with can or bottle through returning them to a deposit middle. There are some of ways to take gain of this opportunity:

Scrounge up all of the cans and bottles you can locate round your home.

look for cans and bottles in trash cans, alongside busy roads, and everywhere that people cling tired (parks, stadiums, and so on.).

Host a bring-your-own-beverage birthday party. when the birthday party's over, acquire all of the bottles and cans and turn them in for coins.

Scrap a junk pile. Metals together with scrap metal, copper, or aluminum can fetch top fees. if you've got a massive pile of scrap in your worn-outside, own a junked camper or different automobile, or understand of an illegal dump web page, you may sort and sell it to a scrap backyard or recycling center in your location.

if your country doesn't have a can/bottle refund machine, you can still promote aluminum cans to a scrap backyard.

Scrap a worthless pc. computer systems are full of precious metals which include metal, aluminum, and gold. if you dismantle vintage computers, you may sort those metals and sell them to a salvage backyard.

If feasible, amass a large range of computers to scrap, to make it really worth your at the same time as. as an instance, provide to take old computers off the palms of a building or school doing giant enhancements or locate junked computers within the classifieds.

Don't scrap appropriate, working computers; what you get for the scrap probably received't be as a lot as you may get with the aid of selling the components or the complete device.

find small paid tasks through apps. There are several money-making apps with a purpose to both pay you for doing advertising responsibilities (which includes scanning products at a grocery store) or connect you with a person who needs a extra big mission (which include completing a survey).

you may not be able to make a great deal money consistent with project this manner. however, you could begin right away and make some money speedy.

live faraway from apps that ask you to do something like pay a price or deliver credit card statistics to sign up to complete surveys. those are nearly constantly scams.

Fill worn-out on line surveys. Many traders use survey responses to find methods of improving their advertising. there are many websites committed that join users to online surveys. these generally only pay at maximum some bucks apiece, however they require little or no effort and may offer fast price.

Amazon's Mechanical Turk software is every other way to make money online by means of answering questions or finishing simple duties. but, the pay is usually very low, often just a few cents per task.

find awareness agencies on your place. recognition organizations are comprised of people that could provide a enterprise, agency, or man or woman with remarks on a product, designtired, idea, and so on. monitor nearby postings or search a website like FindFocusGroups.com to find some on your vicinity that you are eligible to participate in. some of those web sites promote on line-simplest responsibilities, inclusive of serving as an "e-juror" for legal professionals operating on a case. The pay for these obligations can be highly appropriate, and may be distributed quick.

don't forget day exertions. you could post an ad on line or on a bulletin board offering to do unusual jobs. similarly, there are employment companies specializing in brief work. An alternative manner to locate day labor is to go in which other day worker's meet, if you recognize of any, and watch for employers (constructing contractors, landscapers, home owners and small enterprise owners). common atypical jobs people need day people for consist of:

creation

basic workplace obligations

Yardwork (raking leaves, mowing lawns, shoveling snow, cleaning gutters, and so forth.)

selecting up groceries or walking different errands for the aged

Doing chores (cleansing homes, clearing tired an attic or shed, and so on.)

Washing cars

Chapter:3

shifting and/or packing

strive pet sitting. discover buddies who're going tired of town and provide to take care of their pets at the same time as they're gone. professional boarding places tend to be very highly-priced (not to say impersonal and intimidating for a puppy), so your comfy little residence or rental may also appear to be a very exceptional alternative. across the vacations, puppy-boarders top off quickly, which means you may probably charge greater.

recall taking up canine walking people who own puppies but who're too busy to walk them will respect the chance to have their puppies walked. Make a flyer or post an advertisement on on line classifieds forums. Use your cellular telephone for touch; that manner you may get the calls no matter where you are attempting to elevate money!

worn-out to be a babysitter. Babysitting is a commonplace way to make some extra money on the aspect. There are now expert services you may sign up for to be able to join you with those who need a babysitter. For these services, it'll help to bypass a CPR elegance or different certification, or to have a skills or understanding for pleasing kids. but, you might be capable of make money greater speedy simply by babysitting for people you understand, or with the aid of having buddies refer you to others who need a babysitter.

Be a non-public cab driver. agencies consisting of Uber and Lyft have installation services that join drivers with people who need a journey and are willing to pay for it. as a way to take advantage of this possibility quickly, you must own a automobile, have a legitimate motive force's license, and meet different qualifications. it might take a bit little bit of time to get registered as a driving force with the provider, but once you are, there are possibilities to make cash rapid due to the fact these services are in high call for.

turn worntired a road performer. If you may dance, play track, mime, sing, or tell jokes, you may possibly get a few coins by means of acting in public. prepare a great act and find an area to performtired. deliver people a dose of stay entertainment, and with any luck they will reward you with suggestions.

make certain to have a hat, cup, device case, or some thing else equipped for human beings to drop money into.

continually take a look at nearby legal guidelines earlier than performing in a public space, on account that some areas have bans or regulations on this sort of work.

emerge astired a life model. art college students discover ways to draw the human parent by way of reading stay fashions. the ones which might be inclined to pose nude in front of others for as much as half-hour can make money this manner (normally at a consistent with-hour charge).

fashions of all shapes, sizes, and genders are wanted.

you could contact nearby art faculties, faculties, and museums tired possibilities to be a live model for short cash. The website art version tips continues lists of possibilities in each kingdom.

Borrow money. in case you're in critical want of money, you can continually ask to borrow a few from own family or buddies. let them recognise why you need to borrow money, and offer to pay it back within a certain (feasible) timeframe.

beware of loan sharks or other extortionists. look for people that could mortgage you money because they want to help you, now not because they want to make a earnings.

Use your financial institution's overdraft protection. if you have a checking or other account with overdraft safety, you might be capable of intentionally overdraw on the account and take advantage of the brief charge, whilst you are in want of quick coins. The financial institution will first of all cowl the fee, but you'll need to pay it (and probable charges) back.

Use a credit score card's coins increase feature. a few credit cards will allow you to withdraw a positive amount of money through using it at an ATM. this will assist you give you cash in a rush. however, the hobby quotes on coins advances are generally plenty better than the credit card's regular interest charge, that means that you will eventually ought to pay extra.

a few credit playing cards also will let you use cash advances with the aid of writing exams. The interest charges for these are now and again decrease; test along with your bank or credit card issuer for info.

are searching for a payday loan or name mortgage as a closing resort. organizations that provide payday and name loan offerings are generally available, and may be a manner of making brief coins. but, these usually provide extraordinarily high interest charges (on occasion with probabilities in the masses). if you can not pay the loan and any interest lower back in the said timeline, you threat even higher interest costs or, in the case of a identify mortgage, the lack of your vehicle. keep away from these types of loans in all however the maximum dire instances, until you are positive you will be capable of pay the mortgage returned.

As an alternative, you is probably able to ask your organisation for a payday advance.

Panhandle.A panhandler is someone who relies upon at the spontaneous charity of strangers for his or her survival. in case you really want the coins, you might swallow your pride and determine to invite for help. Make a sign that in brief explains your scenario, discover a top area, ask with politeness for money, and say thanks.

ensure that panhandling or begging is permissible in which you live.

the secret to earning profits is not operating at a high-paying process, it's locating innovative answers to humans's issues, and it doesn't take a elaborate degree to do that. To get your creative juices flowing, test worn-out those not unusual and not-so-not unusual methods of lining your pockets. below that, you'll also find greater wellknown monetary recommendation as well as some money-making

purchase underpriced used books. Outfit a cellphone with an ISBN reading app, test the ISBN numbers of books at used bookstores and thrift shops, and evaluate the asking costs with what the books are selling for on a domain like Amazon. each time you get a terrific hit (which received't be often however, since the system is fast, received't take long, both), purchase the e book and resell it on-line. Be discreet abworntired this, as the shop managers possibly received't like what you're doing.

good deal-hunt at backyard and thrift sales. if you have a chunk of knowledge in a selected location (ex. Taxco Mexican silver, action figures, classic countrywide Geographics) or even simply an awesome eye for first-class, visit personal sales early and regularly to discover unexpected deals.

Chapter:4

visit police auctions. you may locate remarkable offers here, and even though might not be capable of resell a car that become involved in a severe crime, you can possibly locate some spectacularly cheap earrings that a person else might be happy to shop for off you.

Refinish ratty furniture. when you have lacquer thinner, sandpaper, stain, and a few craft sense, you may purchase c5ed7369a5a50edae102076547d1405a fixtures and connect it up for a superb resale charge.

Rescue battered timber. Pallets and pallet stock are reasonably-priced (or free) and smooth to return by means of. look for untreated specimens at creation websites, community colleges, buildings underneath preservation, or delivery warehouses and aircraft them down and/or kiln-dry them in a home made kiln-dryer to uncover their hidden beauty. you may then resell the wooden as is or maybe flip it into stunning fixtures. (make sure to put it on the market that the wooden is "reclaimed," as humans are often willing to pay plenty extra for this.)

flip homes or flats. in case you are a accessible(wo)guy with terrific worn-out experience, a information of what's valuable within the production of a home, and belongings you're willing to play with, recollect shopping for, fixing up,

nd reselling actual property. This requires pretty a chunk of up-the front cash and elbow grease, however the payoff can be huge.

sign up with cognizance businesses for your area. studies that you are eligible to participate in pop up sporadically but pay quite properly – regularly greater than $50 for an hour of some time. you may additionally search for consciousness agencies on line but will have to kind through a whole lot of bogus "opportunities" and web sites that ask you to pay up-the front for the privilege of participating earlier than you discover something worthwhile.

take part in clinical studies. If just the notion of this frightens you, recognize that the depth of such studies varies substantially. a few studies ask participants (in particular those with clinical conditions) to test remedies or medicines that may have adverse aspect worn-outcomes, but others ask members to performtired bodily responsibilities without a lasting consequencestired. in case you are able-bodied and paranoid worn-out preserving it that way, you could even participate as a control in a take a look at at a nearby medical studies facility or clinical school.

sell pix. if you have a decent camera and an amazing sense of light, shade, and composition, you could take and sell stock pix – i.e. nondescript snap shots that lend themselves to many programs and are normally used to demonstrate online articles or merchandise – with minimal effort. inventory pictures of locations (a fireplace hydrant, a bare wall close to an exciting tree, or something you might locate as a default history photograph in your pc) are less complicated to take, but stock photos of human beings (i.e. human beings arguing, human beings kissing, people giggling) commonly sell for extra, as they have more uses and require the written felony consent of your subjects. Hunt for a reputable inventory image provider or database a good way to pay you pretty before signing on with all of us.

worn-out net photographs. by using pairing appropriate aesthetic sense and the usage of layworntired or picture-editing software program, you could make and sell heritage graphics for social media pages, net trademarks, or laptop icon packages. if you understand or are willing to research computer programming, severely bear in mind making net pages; programmers can be smooth to come back by means of, however programmers with an eye fixed for splendor are another component altogether.

Make and sell crafts. if you are even a bit bit cunning, keep in mind promoting your items on a domain like Etsy. although you may make extra money on elaborate tasks (ex. an exquisitely woodburned gourd), even labor-light tasks can convey in true cash if you're willing to provide them in excessive quantities. Who is aware of – if you do nicely, you may also be stimulated to begin a crafts enterprise.

worn-out a mystery shopper. this means doing commercial enterprise with various establishments and score their products and services without their expertise. it is able to sound like cake, but take into account that it calls for discreteness, an amazing memory for detail (ex. the call of every man or woman who helped or served you), and sufficient coins for you for you to pay for your buying revel in up-front and then wait to be reimbursed pending the approval of your assessment.

Write product opinions. Many organizations can pay lots extra than two cents on your two cents. Product opinions are a extraordinary way to receives a commission for being opinionated that doesn't require the writing heritage that many other writing jobs do.

whole on line surveys. although tedious, on line surveys are often brief and painless and, for a few bucks at a time, can upload up quick. examine how to Make cash with unfastened online Surveys for greater details.

start a website or blog. certain, opposition within the on line world is steep, however one aspect that makes a very good website online or blog stand apart is the willpower and enthusiasm of its author. masses of websites cognizance too difficult on search engine optimization and keywords, and even as search engine optimization-optimization is withworntired important to help your content make cash, delving into something that actually topics to you may set you aside from your fluff-and-stuff competitors.

start a small business. Being passionate commonly translates to a advanced product and higher provider, which is in particular in demand inside the age of the anonymous, 1-minute on-line overview. worried that there isn't a market in your interests? The fact is that even though you may no longer in my view recognize many those who want what you need to offer, way to the net, there's a large marketplace for area of interest-products (pigeon diapers, chainelectronic mail wedding ceremony clothes, you call it)... and you might simply grow to be being a fashion-setter. To create an online keep, you can either make your own website or, if don't need to self-host, you can sell on eBay or a comparable web page.

Copywriting. Bloggers and commercial enterprise proprietors are obtainable seeking worntired freelance writers to help them with their internet advertising campaigns. If you can write a very good video advertising script, sales replica, press release, product reviews, website content and advertising and marketing copy, you can make money doing exactly that. you may want simple search engine optimization competencies considering that most of those copywriting jobs require a few expertise on how search engines like google and yahoo work. these people are worn-outtired traffic, and they will only lease you if you could deliver that.

Watch and/or stroll your neighbors' pets. Taking a few pooches to the park every week is a good way to have fun, get some worn-out, and meet new human beings, all while making a little coins on the side.

landscape. search for brush-clearing, mowing, or woodcutting jobs, some of which may additionally land you everyday clients. this will prevent money on the same time: in case you are hired to choose up pine needles, use them to mulch your roses, with a view to appreciate their acidity and smothering effect on weeds; in case you are employed to reduce and clear a fallen tree, use it to warmness your house that winter.

Run errands for the elderly. touch your neighborhood network center or church to get in touch with those who want help getting groceries, cleaning their gutters, or attending to the submit office. you would possibly domesticate some lovable friendships at the same time.

discover strange jobs on-line. take a look at tired Craigslist, Fiverr, or Zaarly for interesting or uncommon gigs that come up.

GigWalk: This iPhone app permits you to crew up with corporations posting gigs and get small jobs performedtired for coins. these may be whatever from mystery-purchasing to making deliveries to checking out apps to taking pix. worn-out installation the app, make a profile, and begin worn-outtired gigs in your area.

WeReward: This iPhone and Android app allows you to complete small responsibilities (ex. taking a photograph of yourself together with your favourite beverage or consuming at a brand new established order) for points that translate to coins. although the consistent with-challenge praise is small, there are tens of millions of participating agencies and the points can add up fast. The vicinity-based totally rewards are best if you already have an lively lifestyle and won't ought to pressure yourself to beginning ingesting/consuming worn-out all the time.

CheckPoints: This iPhone and Android app allows you to go to stores and scan objects for points, which you can then use to redeem prizes. that is a available manner to make a touch more at the same time as you do your buying, but note that the rewards are either real merchandise or present certificate – no actual coins.

if you have a manzanita thicket: trim and dry the branches and sell them on-line. believe it or now not, human beings love the usage of them for crafts initiatives. In truth, among the belongings you don't even look twice at ought to be ordered on-line with the aid of humans dwelling in towns don't have access to them.

if you have a curly willow tree: trim, dry, and promote the twisting branches on line to craftspeople or to a local florist, as they're typically used as accent pieces in bouquets.

when you have a pine tree: promote the pinecones that flood your yard every fall. extra lengthy or huge ones make lovely vacation decorations, specially with a simple twist of ribbon.

in case you live by means of the seashore: sell driftwood, which can be used for crafts or, if the pieces are huge and dense, as decorations in marine aquariums.

when you have a pond: pick worntired and dry the cattails earlier than the downy seeds begin dropping and promote them as decorations for bouquets (or maybe bunched together as stand-on my own bouquets). you could also divvy up and promote bits of your water lily, water hyacinth, fairy moss, or every other plant that's doing its satisfactory to overtake your pond besides.

if you have a tree drowning in mistletoe: reduce the mistletoe down, flip it into festive, ribbon-wrapped bunches, and sell it around the vacations.

in case you are promoting some thing which you realize or can confirm hasn't been handled:you may even promote it it as being organic, which might heighten interest and let you growth the rate.

if you don't have get entry to to any of these items: receives a commission to gather them from other human beings. masses of people could luckily lease a person to reduce their Manzanita forest or wade into a pond and spoil apart their water-lily thicket, that means you may make cash from each accumulating and promoting your product.

grow to be a moving advertisement. "Wrap" your car in an commercial, go worn-outapproximately your typical shuttle, and receives a commission month-to-month to do it. (a few car-wrappers in San Francisco make as lots as $400 a month doing this,however of path this varies depending on how huge a city you live in and while / how regularly you're making your trip.) you can additionally get paid to put on a organization's emblem t-blouse around (mainly if you put on it somewhere conspicuous, like at your school; see ShirtsInSchools.com as one example).

lease worn-out a area. if you have a spare room, an unused parking spot or driveway in a busy part of town, or maybe an empty lot which you wouldn't mind seeing transformed into an city garden, hire it worn-out and experience an extra monthly paycheck.

try affiliate marketing. this means selling someone else's products or services for pay with out honestly sporting an inventory. there are numerous ways of incorporating affiliate advertising into your website/ weblog/web page along with banner ads (which can be typically ineffective, as humans tend to avoid these), linked articles (that are quite successful whilst the item content is considerate and doesn't seem spammy), and product-placement videos (which may be very successful whilst completed through human beings with air of mystery or an awesome humorousness). you could even become an associate marketer with out a website. primary methods of making a living thru of affiliate advertising encompass:

price-consistent with-click: you receives a commission a very small amount every time a person clicks from your content material onto the advertiser's website; top for high-traffic content

value-per-lead: you receives a commission a chunk more each time someone symptoms up or fills a shape with the advertiser way to your content material

fee-in step with-acquisition: you receives a commission a (fixed or percentage) commission on every occasion someone makes a buy with the advertiser because of your content; good for focused, 86f68e4d402306ad3cd330d005134dac content

sell CDs and/or DVDs. again up your collection on a laptop or externaltired difficult drive, then promote the original discs. You'll make short coins and store space at the identical time. if you have prized collections (boxed units, constrained-release variants, and many others.), promote those personally for what they're well worth; otherwise, promote your discs very moderately (recollect, your potential customers can also get the exact songs they need instantly by way of downloading them for greenback or less apiece). Even for a mere $four every, a considerable collection of CDs can haul in a tidy – sum.

promote hair, plasma, or different body components/fluids. lengthy, wholesome, untreated hair may be bought for a spread of purposes (inclusive of excessive-quit wig- and extension-making) and earn you anywhere from numerous hundred to several thousand dollars relying on coloration, fitness, and period. Plasma can be "donated" (for reimbursement) provided which you are antique, healthful, and heavy enough to qualify. Sperm may be donated, but you usually need to recognize (and be capable of document) a honest quantity of records worn-outtired your dad and mom in addition to your clinical history to be eligible. but be cautious; as an example, donating eggs is regularly tworn-outed as a quick, high-income clinical method, but the process is truly requires that the player undergo hormonal and clinical remedy, obtain regular checkups and ultrasounds, and abstain from intercourse and intoxicants, all of which take weeks or even months before the eggs are even eligible for removal. The elimination technique itself is invasive and lasts abworntired 30 minutes.do not forget your alternatives very carefully earlier than taking on anything like this.

Use the law of supply and demand on your benefit. maximum folks are familiar with the regulation of supply and call for--the more there may be of some thing, the inexpensive it's miles; conversely, the rarer the services or products, the extra luxurious it's miles. however, apart from when we get to a toy save earlier than sunrise to get on-line for the today's fad toy that kids can't get enough of, we don't honestly observe the regulation of supply and call for to our personal lives--mainly our careers. as an example, if you're meaning to do something that many, many different people want to do (a lot in order that they do it for free, as a hobby) then it will likely be a ways greater challenging if you want to make cash doing it. however, if you do something that most people don't need to do, or if you get very good at doing some thing most people do not do all that properly, then you could make an entire lot extra money. In other phrases, pick a career in pharmacy over photography.

if your profession rworntired is going nowhere, resign gracefully and transfer careers.studies occupations to find worntired how plenty they pay and what their destiny tiredlook is (within the U.S., you could find this data within the Bureau of exertions data Occupational Outlook guide). locate an profession that pays well, and make investments inside the education and/or education to get you that activity. look for employers that provide aggressive salaries and sufficient opportunity for advancement.

in case your goal is to make sufficient money to retire early, prioritize earning potential over task satisfaction, since you plan on getting worn-out of the rat race early, besides.remember the types of jobs that pay particularly well in trade for difficult work, little psychological delight, and a punishing life-style, which include investment banking, income, and engineering. If you can maintain your charges low and do that for worn-out 10 years, you can store a nest egg for a modest however younger retirement, or to complement your profits whilst you do some thing you actually love doing however does not pay tons. however remember the fact that behind schedule gratification calls for clear purpose-placing and robust self-control.

understand that time is cash. This important piece of recommendation is attributed to Benjamin Franklin, who become an performedtired American inventor, journalist, printer, diplomat, and statesman--the remaining multitasker. Your capability to control it slow (and prevent procrastinating) is a vital ingredient to your capacity to make cash. whether or not you've got a activity or are self-hired, keep music of what you're spending it slow on. Ask yourself "Which of these activities make the most money, and which ones are a waste of time?" Do greater of the previous and less of the latter, easy as that. while you're specializing in excessive-precedence responsibilities, get the process worn-out nicely, and get the activity performedtired rapid. through running effectively, you are giving your company or customers greater time, and they may respect you for it. take into account that time is a limited aid which you're constantly investing. Will your investments repay?

Jack up your charges. if you're imparting a talent, product or service that is in high demand and coffee supply, and you're making the maximum of some time, you need to be making right cash. regrettably, there are many folks who are too humble or apprehensive to demand that they receives a commission consequently. it is the pushovers in existence who get taken benefit of and exploited, so in case you suppose you might be certainly one of them, analyze how to prevent being a people pleaser. if you work for someone else, ask for a pay enhance or get a merchandising, and if none of that pans tired, revisit your profession options as described formerly. in case you're self-employed, the first component to do is to ensure your customers and customers pay up on time--this by myself can drastically enhance your earnings. take a look at your prices and quotes towards the ones of your competition--are you undercutting them? Why? in case you're presenting a superior product or service, you have to be getting at least the common, unless your profitability depends on mass production, wherein case you're in all likelihood making a variety of money and would not be studying this newsletter besides!

Be proactive. recall Murphy's law: "whatever can pass incorrect will go wrong." Make plans, whole with as many calculations as feasible, then assume the whole lot which can go wrong. Then make contingency or backup plans for each situation. do not leave something to success. in case you're writing a business plan, as an instance, do your fine to estimate whilst you will break even, then multiply that point frame by using 3 to get a greater realistic date; and after you've diagnosed all of the fees, add 20% to that for costs a good way to arise which you did not expect. Your excellent defense against Murphy's regulation is to count on the worst, and brace your self. the best quantity of insurance can be something well worth considering. keep in mind the advice of Louis Pasteur, a French chemist who made numerous terrific breakthroughs within the reasons and prevention of sickness: "success favors the organized mind."

Redefine wealth. In research of millionaires, humans are surprised to research that most millionaires aren't docs, attorneys, and corporate leaders with massive homes and fancy cars; they may be individuals who religiously stay below their method and make investments the excess into belongings, instead of liabilities.[4] As you take the above steps to make extra cash, remember the fact that elevated earnings does no longer always identical improved wealth. most people who flaunt their wealth in reality have a low net really worth because their debt to asset ratio is high--in different phrases, they owe an entire lot more money than they sincerely have. all of the preceding steps have outlined aggressive strategies for making money, however you may by no means get anywhere when you have a hole on your pocket.

they say that a penny stored is a penny earned. sincerely, when you consider which you pay taxes on every penny you earn, you clearly do make more money by way of savingthan with the aid of increasing your profits, especially if the more earnings will increase your tax rate dramatically. for instance, let's assume you have a desire among saving $100 or incomes an additional $one hundred. in case you pay 15% taxes, then while you earn an $a hundred, you handiest get $eighty five. however when you keep $one hundred off of your current price range, you keep all of it. To sweeten the deal similarly, in case you take gain of compound interest as determined in maximum financial savings money owed, over time you will start earning money on the amount stored plus preceding interest paid on that quantity saved. it is going to be pennies at the beginning, but sooner or later the quantity will multiply exponentially.

Chapter:5

Take gain of tax legal guidelines if you're self-hired. cash saved on taxes is still cash stored. you will be capable of deduct lots of your enterprise costs (use of your house, use of your car, workplace resources, and many others.) in case you maintain desirable information. you can additionally qualify for tax breaks, along with deducting your medical health insurance charges to your tax go back. these legal guidelines are in place to inspire commerce and commercial enterprise boom, so don't forget abworntired their benefits specifically if you want to make cash.

in case you're no longer self-employed and work for a employer, tired in the event that they have a retirement plan. if you're fortunate, employers will from time to time healthy contributions you are making into a retirement fund. Retirement plans also often have the benefit of being tax-deferred. The longer you get to preserve your money (and make hobby on it) the better. it's in no way too early to start making plans for retirement.

know the distinction between an asset and a legal responsibility. The dividing line is whether or not it puts money on your pocket, or takes it tired.[5] As plenty as you like your own home, for instance, it's far a liability instead of an asset because you placed more money into it than you get worn-out of it (unless you're flipping it or renting it tired). something money you shop, invest it in property including stocks, mutual finances, patents, copyrighted works--some thing that generates interest or royalties. finally, you would possibly get to the factor wherein your property are doing the work for you, and all you have to do is take a seat there and make cash!

be careful for inflation chipping away at your assets. we've got all heard an elderly man or woman describe the buying power of a coin of their day. Inflation maintains to make brand new cash really worth less within the future. To win the race in opposition to time and inflation, learn how to make investments your money inside the right places. A financial savings account might assist you to preserve up with inflation; however, to stay in advance of the sport you will need to invest in bonds, shares, or a few different funding that returns above the common rate of inflation (presently three%-four%).

Ask your parents if they may pay you for doing extra chores. you're probably already anticipated to do chores across the house and assist tired your own family at no cost. if you want a little greater pocket change, however, ask your dad and mom if there is some thing else you could do for a small charge. as an instance, maybe your mom truly hates folding laundry and would be willing to pay $five every week for you to do it instead. whatever it is, allow your parents understand you're inclined to take on extra work for a chunk of allowance.

ensure you're capable of do anything you settle to do. in case you recognise your mother and father like a chore worn-out a sure way, don't cut corners - do it properly, and they may even agree to provide you a enhance in the destiny!

make sure you are able to do whatever you settle to do. if you realize your parents like a chore worn-out a sure way, don't reduce corners - do it well, and they may even agree to present you a enhance in the destiny!

provide some thing it is appropriate for the climate. cold beverages or popsicles will sell better on a hot day than on a wet day. If it's too bloodless or miserable worntired to do much enterprise, maintain off and await a better day.

preserve your expenses down. with a purpose to flip a profit on what you are promoting, pick to promote an item it truly is cheaper to make. Lemonade is a traditional due to the fact all of its substances (water, sugar, lemons or lemon juice listen, and ice) are pretty cheap and clean to reap. Popsicles are some other favorite because they can be sold in huge quantities from the store!

installation on public property. you could installation your stand on a sidewalk, public park, or different place that is not owned through a non-public individual. Doing this could assist you keep away from accusations of trespassing. Be conscious, even though, that some large metropolitan parks might require you to get a permit to promote there.

put it up for sale your rate. Get a huge piece of paper, cardboard or poster paper, and write what you are promoting and what kind of one serving expenses. as an instance, you would possibly write "LEMONADE, 25 CENTS". Set a fair rate point, and make it something you would be inclined to pay your self; if you're not certain what's honest, ask your mother and father or any other trustworthy person.

Have someplace comfy to maintain your cash. discover a lockbox, coin handbag, wallet, or envelope to hold your income secure and amassed.

Do ordinary jobs around your community. Mowing lawns, babysitting, raking leaves, snow shoveling, washing automobiles, and bathing pets are all examples of services that many people are willing to pay someone else to do. If you may do some of this stuff and you've got a few spare time, knock on the doorways of own family individuals or associates you know nicely, and provide your offerings.

only paintings for human beings you already know or your parents know nicely; by no means paintings for strangers.

Be sincere. people like to know that whoever's operating round their domestic or with their children can be relied on, and they could also be willing to pay extra for that peace of mind. Be fair and honest in all your dealings, and in no way steal; these characteristics will pay off later.

Be inclined to barter. you might have two associates who need their sidewalks shoveled, but one might be willing to pay $five consistent with week at the same time as any other will pay simplest $3. If the neighbor who is paying you much less is elderly, residing on a set income, disabled or otherwise strapped for cash, bear in mind accepting the lower charge in order to build your customers. recollect, that individual who can pay you much less might later advise your offerings to someone else willing to pay greater.

.constructing a internet site is a first-rate manner to percentage your ideas and mind with the sector. but if you've in no way accomplished one, it can seem daunting. there is all that http-dot-some thing and and and how do you get pictures and textual content in there? nicely worry now not, this newsletter will help you to grasp the intricacies right away!

Get inspired. examine web sites with great designs and think abworntired why they're notable designs. It generally comes right down to the data, assets, links, and pages being laid out in a manner that is straightforward to see and use. To get thoughts tired the way to layworntired your own web site, have a look at websites which do comparable matters to get thoughts worn-outapproximately wherein you ought to positioned distinctive kinds of content material.

live realistic for your abilties.

Ease of get entry to is the maximum important factor. in case you do not have a certain piece of statistics effortlessly seen, make sure that getting to that records is very logical.

normally the easier the designtired, the fewer the pages, the higher.

pick worntired a subject and cause. if you already have a fairly true idea tired what your website will attention on, bypass this step. If now not, right here are a few matters to help you discern that tired. First, keep in mind that there are billions of people at the internet, and a big percentage have web sites. if you limit yourself to some thing that hasn't been worn-out, you'll by no means get worn-out.

when you assume, "net," what is the primary aspect that comes to your mind? E-trade? song? news? Socializing? running a blog? the ones are all precise places to start.

you can create a internet site it truly is dedicated to your favourite band, and have a talk area in which humans can speak abworntired it.

Chapter:6

you can build a web page on your circle of relatives, but be careful worn-outtired things like this. The net is full of unsavory characters and statistics you positioned up worn-outapproximately your circle of relatives may want to become being used towards you. recollect adding password protection to your personal own family website.

if you're a information junkie, or need some thing less filtered than conventional media, construct a internet site and get publicly available feeds from news vendors which includes Reuters, BBC, AP, and others. build your own custom designed news aggregator (what used to head by way of the quaint name of "newspaper"), then see and display all the news it is in shape to digitize.

if you're creative at writing then you can begin a weblog wherein you may write worn-out something you need and appeal to monthly readers!

acquire the content material. There are lots of different kinds of content and many have their very own issues. you may need to parent tired what's first-class for your internet site and your wishes. a few things to consider such as:

a store. in case you need to promote things, you may need to figure worn-out how you need the gadgets to be available. when you have particularly few things to sell, you might need to do not forget having a store with a web hosting provider. Society6, Amazon, and Cafepress are all well-mounted shop hosts which permit you to sell a diffusion of items and set your own prices.

Chapter:7

Media. Do you need to show videos? music? Do you need to host your personal documents or do you need them hosted some other place? Ytiredube and SoundCloud are superb examples of web hosting alternatives, however you'll need to ensure that the manner you worn-out your internet site permits these media sorts to display correctly.

pix. Are you a photographer? An artist? if you plan on placing authentic pics to your website, you might want to use a formattired which can help keep them from getting stolen. make sure the photographs are tremendously small or that they're hidden at the back of some Flash code, which will keep them from being easily saveable.

Widgets. those are mini-programs which run in your website, normally that will help you preserve track of who visits, what they may be searching worntired, and where they're from. you could additionally discover widgets for booking appointments, showing a calendar, etc. worn-out what is probably beneficial for you (just make sure the widget comes from a good supply).

contact records. Do you want to have contact statistics for your website? to your very own safety, you need to be cautious worn-out what form of statistics you have available. You have to by no means show things like your house cope with or domestic cellphone quantity, as records like this will be used to thieve your identity. you could need to installation a PO field or a unique e mail deal with for human beings to touch you at, if you do not have a commercial enterprise cope with.

Draw a waft chart. For most of the people, the website begins on the domestic page. this is the page that everyone sees after they first visit www.yourSite.com. however in which do they cross from there?

if you spend a while thinking abworntired how people might engage with your site, you will have a much simpler time down the road when you are making navigation buttons and links.

Plan for user devices and situations. In latest years, smartphones and drugs have become relatively famous platforms for browsing the net, and that they require web sites to be designed for them. in case you really want to make a internet site in an effort to stand the check of time and be handy to the highest wide variety of viewers, plan on making exclusive versions of your web page for distinctive gadgets, or plan to use a responsive layworntired that adjusts as essential.

decide what approach or tool you will use to construct it. when you have the basic idea down and feature a plan for how it will likely be laid tired, the subsequent to think abworntired is how you will construct it. The alternatives appear endless, and people will attempt to sell you this or that 'remarkable' software, and each different issue which you "worn-out must have" on your website, however the fact is that there are some wonderful gear for building websites, and one of them may be first-rate-perfect for your state of affairs and wishes.

Chapter:8

construct it your self. this is the first alternative. when you have a internet site-constructing software like Adobe Dreamweaver, it isn't very tough to create a internet site from scratch. you would possibly need to do some coding but do not panic! HTML looks complicated, however it is like listening to Shakespeare—it is difficult before everything, however when you get the feel of it, it is now not that difficult.

pros: website design software program simplifies the process of building websites through letting you drag-and-drop pictures, text, buttons, films, and some thing else you could worn-outtired, usually with out ever having to dig into HTML. Many internet designtired packages will also will let you create web sites particularly in your clever smartphone or pad. if you are constructing a primary, personal website, that is surely a tremendous manner to move.

Cons: there is a gaining knowledge of curve, and although you do not must dig into HTML, it's no longer absolutely geek-free. if you are in a rush, this might not be the pleasant solution. perhaps the largest con, though, is that if you aren't a picture dressmaker, you may want to end up with a web page that hurts the eyes. To mollify this really, there are some of free templates within the applications, and at the internet, however be aware abworntired your barriers—when you have any!

Use a content control machine (CMS). this is the 2d choice. WordPressis an instance of a first rate choice for building websites. It facilitates you create net pages and blog posts quickly and easily, set up the menus, permit and manipulate user remarks, and has hundreds of subject matters and plugins that you may pick worntired from and use for free. Drupal and Joomla are other worntired CMS options. as soon as the CMS is hosted, you can manipulate your website online from everywhere (in the world) that has an internet connection.

pros: Very easy to use, brief to get started worntired with one click set up, and lots of alternatives for the amateur (with sufficient intensity for more skilled users).

Cons: some subject matters are restricting, and not all are loose.

Chapter:9

rent a professional. this is the fourth and very last choice. if you are not as much as designing your very own internet site, or learning new coding languages—specifically for more superior sites—hiring a expert can be your first-class alternative. before you hire, ask to peer a portfolio in their paintings, and take a look at their references carefully.

sign up your domain name. if you're on a price range, there are techniques for buying a cheap domain call. find a area name that is straightforward to recollect and smooth to spell. in case you use domains ending with .com, you'll worn-out to be with greater visitors, however most of the clean ones are taken, so be innovative!

look to network answers, GoDaddy, or check in.com are top in US and uk2.internet if you're inside the uk to investigate and discover the precise domain name in your website. Wordpress also consists of a feature wherein you may use a call it is tagged with their web page, as an instance, mywebsite.wordpress.com. but if the name you worn-outtired is likewise available as a .com, they'll notify you while you sign on.

you should buy domains in the event that they were "parked" or are for sale online through enterprise sales sites. it is a great concept to get prison and monetary recommendation earlier than purchasing an steeply-priced domain call.

look at your internet site. earlier than you post your web page, it's wise to check it thoroughly. most internet worn-out software has a way to check your web page with out taking it on line. look for missing tags, broken links, seo, and website design flaws. these are all elements which can also have an effect on your website's visitors and sales. you can also generate a unfastened complete-functioning website map to publish to search engines like Google, in a matter of mins.

take a look at your internet site. when you finish your internet site, do usability trying out. you can do this with the aid of asking some friends or own family individuals to strive it tired. supply them a selected project like "edit your profile" or "purchase an alpaca sweater from the bargains web page." take a seat at the back of them and watch them navigate—do now not help them. you may in all likelihood discover areas where you need to improve navigation or make clear a few instructions. Alternately use something like zurb.com to person take a look at on unique demographics for extraordinary sorts of engagement. whilst checking out a internet site in 2014 it is turning into critical to keep the platform in mind and make sure the internet site is usable from smartphones and capsules as well as computers.

preserve a list of things you notice that seem tough or non-intuitive for the person.

launch it! worn-outtired an internet host and upload your internet site. Your net host may additionally have an FTP characteristic, or you may down load your own FTP software like FileZilla or CyberDuck. if you employed a professional to layworntired the internet site, they have to have the ability to take care of this for you (but it still can pay to invite questions so you apprehend what's occurring).

word that there are methods to host your very own internet site free of charge.

slender down your idea. if you're doing this for money, which thoughts stand to make the maximum earnings? Which thoughts require the most dedication? Which thoughts appear like they had be amusing to pursue? you may be spending time operating in your website, so worn-out the idea you are maximum captivated with (this is additionally profitable and realistic for you).

worn-outline your goals, and work to attain them. The website you create may be for amusing, it may be for profit, or some combination of the 2. knowing your expectancies makes it tons simpler each to worn-out your internet site, and to tune and make feel of the results.

Be equipped for competition. content material web sites require much less investment however in addition they face extra competition, considering that anybody can start a content material website. To make cash from this form of website online, you offer information and generate income from the visitors you acquire thru advertising, such as through Google AdSense. with a view to optimize AdSense, you will ought to write your content purposefully and make it exciting in order that human beings come to your site. Use specific keywords directed at human beings attempting to find specific terms too; simply do not get carried away with this factor or the content material may go through and readers may not love it.

Be ready for responsibility. eCommerce sites, which promote merchandise, will want extra renovation and interest. you may want to reflect onconsideration ontired transport, income, taxes, SSL, stock updates, and the entirety that a person with a brick-and-mortar storefront might ought to control. A device for spark off answering of questions and coping with court cases is critical when selling merchandise online; many companies additionally offer telephone assist, which you may worn-outsource offshore if want be.

If the intention is just to feature a movement of income, you can also promote different people's products via associate programs, letting you earn cash without investing in product or traumatic tired transport.

realize the audience or market you want to reach. Which types of human beings will your website serve? behavior market studies to figure tired greater worn-out your target market. things to recognize or find worntired consist of: What do they do? How antique are they? What are their other pursuits? All of this records can assist make your website plenty extra useful. however, be cautious of assuming that your site is only concentrated on one organization--usually look ahead to trends that show other types of humans turning into involved, so that you can cater for his or her hobbies too and make the maximum of latest opportunities.

Do key-word research. that is vital to determine whether humans are trying to find subjects that are relevant on your website online and may be beneficial for studying more worn-outapproximately your ability customers. creating a conscious attempt to comprise in-demand key phrases into the site can also help you get a better search engine ranking. There are gear available from Google (ex. google.com/trends/ and google.com/insights/search/#), Overture, and 1/3-birthday celebration software program developers that may make the keyword studies system easier.

Sprinkle the key phrases you have chosen worn-out your text, however now not insofar because it hurts the first-class of your content material.

growing pages which are optimized for the search engines like google and yahoo will help you get your website observed which is simply greater important than layworntired. What properly is a website that no person sees?

promote it. Now that it is available, you want human beings to come, so allow them to recognise!

post your site to predominant serps. There are websites to be able to do this for you, or you could do it yourself.

inform your pals. Tweet worn-out it—constantly! upload it on your fb reputation updates, publish images of it on Flickr, add it to your LinkedIn account—everywhere and anywhere is the key right here. The extra human beings coming on your site, the higher.

Use an 1ec5f5ec77c51a968271b2ca9862907d cope with together with your domain. go to other websites that complement (not compete with) yours, and provide to exchange links or guest weblog/write. post constructively on blogs and forums, and placed your URL to your signature.

Use article advertising and marketing. developing seo-optimized articles and posting them to different sites is a now and again a beneficial way to create lower back-hyperlinks for your internet site. this might assist you to reinforce your internet site's search engine ranking however constantly preserve abreast of search engine updates that regularly impact seo strategies and may render them much less beneficial or even downgrade your site's ranking.

offer quality content material and service. most of all, listen for your readers and clients and study from their revel in together with your website.

Take constructive comments significantly. different band contributors, fans, and buddies may also all have less complicated navigation ideas.

worn-outconsider your goal market or audience: their desires, their frustrations, their situations. As much as feasible, are seeking for to make their lives simpler or greater knowledgeable.

Chapter:10

recognize the reality of getting cash by means of finding cash. although you could make a profitable amount of money this way, don't mistake this as an efficient money-making venture. deal with it as a recreation or a interest and you may have a much higher time. recognize that maximum days, you won't discover a full-size sum of money.

stay clean out there. money is one of the filthiest things that people contact on a regular basis, germ-sensible. it really is as it's treated by using such a lot of people, going from man or woman to person all the time. when you're out cash searching, keep a bottle of hand sanitizer with you and don't be stingy with it. in particular after you check places like public restrooms and parking lots.

Have a place to shop what you locate. when you're just out going about your business and also you manifest upon money, you may just store it to your pocket or purse. but if you go out with the goal of looking for cash, it is nice to have something to preserve it in while you're out, like a coin handbag or a small bag.

it's also well worth having an area to save your located cash at home, like a piggy bank or something equivalent.

determine how you will turn your trade into cash.There are 3 most important strategies for turning cash into cash. you may use a system designed for any such issue, like Coinstar. you could take it to your bank and use their coin counting device if they have one. Or you could retrieve a few trade roll paper from your financial institution and roll the change up your self, then trade it at the bank.

whether or no longer using your bank to trade your cash for cash is your pleasant option depends on some factors. a few banks have coin counting machines and some don't. Of those that do, a few require a fee to apply and a few don't. a few banks will offer you with coin roll paper without cost and some do not.

take into account that at the same time as Coinstar is the most handy technique, they also take eight to 10 percent of your income for his or her services. this will be averted though, in case you use their gift card application instead of turning inside the voucher for cold tough coins.

locate forgot money on your fixtures. humans regularly empty their pockets in their bed room, which means that under your mattress and bedside fixtures is a top notch first location to appearance. Of route, sofa cushions and chair cushions are some other brilliant vicinity for free alternate to be found. check under and around all the fixtures in your house.

don't forget about your washing gadget and dryer. human beings regularly depart cash in their garments on twist of fate after which wash them, leaving cash and coins in and across the washing system and dryer.

check all your clothes and bags. it is no atypical incidence to from time to time locate cash in the pair of pants you're wearing that you had completely forgotten about. So do your self a prefer and are seeking out all the forgotten cash now. go through all your pants and jacket pockets for money. And whilst you're at it, undergo any purses and luggage you operate as nicely.

look through your vehicle. anywhere you sit down down frequently is a top region to look for lost trade. Make a sweep thru your vehicle, under the seats and within the seat cushions. cash tend to collect in places which might be frequented regularly but by no means very well seemed via.

look for cash in places where cash is treated often.This consists of shops, restaurants, public phones, public transportation, and bars. maintain an eye fixed at the floors of those locations, and you may be surprised by how tons cash you can spot. try to be at least a touch discrete approximately this even though. You don't need people wondering why you're roaming round a restaurant along with your returned bent and your eyes glued to the floor.

Be careful to now not pick up cash that turned into just dropped. you would possibly find a stray dollar in the nook of a bar, however if it turned into simply dropped via someone, return it them if they may be no longer selecting it up themselves. The intention is to collect money left behind, now not steal.

Pay cautious attention to sides and corners, where coins can effortlessly roll out of sight and out of the way.

take a look at parking masses and bleachers. look into beneath bleachers at carrying activities, gala's, and different venues with open-bottomed bleachers. additionally check vehicle parking plenty, in particular those of night time golf equipment and bars. achieve this in the morning hours, before visitors starts transferring. it's outstanding what human beings will drop whilst they are inebriated, worn-out, and distracted.

on every occasion you need to go to a shop, park a long way from the store, so that you can look for money at the floor as you stroll.

Pay more interest to self-pay parking plenty and drive-throughs. people will reach from their vehicle window to pay, and often drop coins to the ground. the majority may not hassle to get out in their automobile to acquire this change.

strive merchandising machines. take a look at the coin return slots in vending machines. appearance in the back of and below them for alternate that has rolled out of sight. most people will no longer bend down and rummage underneath a vending system to find a coin they have lost.

keep a watch at the sidewalk. appearance down alleyways, and regularly-used footpaths where human beings may drop their spare change. this is an easy factor to do when you're out on different commercial enterprise. it's just about making a addiction of being observant of the floor and what you may encounter.

test bathrooms and public furniture. test behind the public rest room seat. human beings must drop their trousers, and some thing may want to come out of these wallet, along with exchange or bills. also, appearance at the back of the cushions of the couch, and seats, that you find within the foyer and bars of a lodge. this can be done by way of discreetly jogging your hand in the back of the cushions once you sit down.

Chapter:11

take a look at numerous distinct web sites' pay fees. simple stock photo web sites like Dreamstime, freedigitalphotos.internet, and Shutterstock are famous choices for newbie photographers, even as the professionals often select Getty images or Corbis. every of those sites has a distinctive pay charge, but maximum sites provide as a minimum 30% commission. make certain to check each web site's commission fee earlier than you sign on.

regularly, the most famous websites pay the smallest fee. whether or not or no longer you need to sell speedy for less money or wait longer for more money is as much as you!

check the website online's requirements and themes to keep away from rejected pics. each web site has its personal necessities for download first-class and its very own focus on issues. Your photographs may not be ordinary in case you don't comply with the website online's unique requirements. make certain your pix meet the requirements and match the website online's theme before you put up them.

for instance, Dreamstime requires not less than 3 megapixels for down load size, and they also decide upon commercial enterprise-orientated images.

sign up for an account. Registration with the website online that you choose is generally unfastened. If the web page isn't always unfastened, you could want to reconsider the usage of them unless the price is quite cheap and a one-time fee. be sure to examine the website online's instructions cautiously, due to the fact there's frequently essential records about fee and copyright troubles included.

review and complete the fee portion of your account. most websites can pay you via Paypal, even though some websites may pay via test via the mail. you may need to provide the e-mail deal with related to your Paypal account, at the side of any additional facts they require. if you do not have a Paypal account, set one up. whilst you're paid varies from website online to web site. some handiest pay you while you request a cash-out, and others pay on a particular day of the month.

make certain you are registering with a reputable website online before giving them your account statistics or home deal with.

recall registering for a couple of websites. Registering for more than one websites can can help you make extra money, however be cautious! if you sell an image on one website, you may have to get rid of it on all of your other websites. also, some sites will provide extraordinary contracts that pay you extra in case you most effective promote your pics to them. study all the excellent print earlier than registering to multiple websites!

broaden a diverse portfolio of digital pix. in case you only have four or five essential subjects to your pix, they may simplest enchantment to a sure type of consumer. while you may still make cash this way, it's better to have a numerous collection of pix with many unique topics and tones. The extra human beings your photos attraction to, the more money you'll make.

choose regularly occurring pix to make the maximum cash.common photographs enchantment to the biggest audience, so these pictures will sell more regularly than area of interest or unusual pix. go through your virtual portfolio and choose out general photos with mass attraction. as an example, photographs of vegetation and landscapes paintings nicely.

single-problem pictures, like a bookcase of old books, a windmill, or a wine bottle, additionally paintings nicely.

some thing commercial enterprise or office-orientated commonly does properly.

frequent tones additionally promote well on inventory websites. as an instance, photographs that appearance vintage.

choose images which might be high first-class for the first-class consequences. maximum stock sites have guidelines approximately decision, size, file layout, and so on. make sure your pix adhere to the ones policies in order that they may not be rejected. If the website you're the usage of would not have set necessities, customers are much more likely to purchase excessive first-class pics with top decision.

Use handiest your very exceptional paintings. pick out pix with crisp element and balanced coloration.

for example, photos that are blurry or excessive contrast would not be appropriate picks.

upload your photographs to the inventory web page. ensure your preferred snap shots comply with all of the web site's policies and necessities, consisting of picture length, decision, document kind, and so on. in case your web page lets you post photos in specific categories, ensure your photos healthy the cate

Tag your pix with applicable tags to appear in site searches. whilst you add your pix to websites, they'll be amongst hundreds of other snap shots. contemplating tags for each picture will assist them come up first in searches. choose more than one tags for every picture.

for example, if you upload a photograph of the seaside, your tags would possibly consist of words like "beach," "a laugh," "sunny day," "sand," "surfing," or "tropical."

gories to growth income.

experiment with the usage of a mixture of widely wide-spread tags and precise tags. customary tags are the maximum famous ones because they're the most looked for. the usage of everyday tags will get your pics in the front of the the general public. precise tags can get your images in front of a one-of-a-kind institution of people. Use a mix of each, so humans attempting to find some thing precise can find you, and so can people searching for general terms.

as an example, if your seashore photo is of a boardwalk in New Jersey, use familiar tags like "seashore," "boardwalk," "ocean view" and so on.

Then encompass particular tags like "New Jersey," "Asbury Park," and "South point Boardwalk."

keep away from the use of snap shots with visible or recognizable manufacturers in them. the use of photos like those can get you into trouble, because you'll be earning profits off of a person else's brand without their know-how or approval. maximum stock picture websites have regulations in opposition to using snap shots like this. keep away from them altogether to keep away from running into troubles.

as an instance, an photo of a Ford Mustang convertible or Campbell's soup can might be beside the point to upload and promote.

avoid the usage of snap shots offering company logos, stills from movies, or anything else in the beginning made by means of some thing else.

avoid the use of photographs with humans or properties in them. Any character that looks to your inventory pix need to sign a launch shape before the picture may be sold. The same is going for snap shots depicting someone's non-public property, along with a local storefront or your neighbor's barn. you would want to tune down an appropriate criminal forms and get them signed every time you used an photograph like this, which would be a trouble. In some cases, it is able to even be impossible.

you may down load model launch bureaucracy on line, or write up your personal.

Take all of your photographs yourself to get an automated copyright. according to international copyright law, the photographer mechanically owns the copyrights to whatever they take themselves. You don't ought to register or sign on for the copyright in case you were the one working the camera.

One exception is snap shots taken while you have been hired by a enterprise as a photographer. as an instance, if you are a photographer operating for a newspaper, the newspaper owns the photos you are taking on the job.

Registering your copyright isn't required, however it's regularly an awesome concept--it can prevent human beings from stealing your paintings.